POLLUTED WATER AND YOUR VITAL ORGANS

Bridget Heos

rosen publishing's
rosen central®

Published in 2013 by The Rosen Publishing Group, Inc.
29 East 21st Street, New York, NY 10010

Copyright © 2013 by The Rosen Publishing Group, Inc.

First Edition

Library of Congress Cataloging-in-Publication Data

Heos, Bridget.
Polluted water and your vital organs/Bridget Heos.—1st ed.
     p. cm.—(Incredibly disgusting environments)
Includes bibliographical references and index.
ISBN 978-1-4488-8412-4 (library binding)—
ISBN 978-1-4488-8424-7 (pbk.)—
ISBN 978-1-4488-8428-5 (6-pack)
1. Water—Pollution—Health aspects—United States. 2. Water—
Purification—United States. 3. Drinking water—Contamination—
Health aspects—United States. 4. Drinking water—Purification—
United States. I. Title.
RA592.A1H46 2013
363.739'4—dc23

2012018880

Manufactured in the United States of America

CPSIA Compliance Information: Batch #W13YA: For further information, contact Rosen Publishing, New York, New York, at 1-800-237-9932.

CONTENTS

INTRODUCTION

Jennifer Hall-Massey, of Prenter, West Virginia, doesn't let her sons play in the bath water. She gets them out as quickly as possible because the tap water in their home causes painful rashes. One of her sons also has multiple tooth cavities from when the family used to drink the water. More troubling, within a ten-house span, six neighbors developed brain tumors, including Hall-Massey's younger brother, who passed away. In contrast, the national average for people diagnosed with brain cancer is only 6.4 in 100,000. Community wide, there is a cluster of brain tumors, and Hall-Massey believes these and other health problems are due to polluted drinking water. Others agree. Tests have confirmed that the water contains levels of chemicals such as arsenic, barium, and lead that federal regulations say could cause cancer.

When Hall-Massey and more than five hundred other community members sued nearby coal companies, including Massey Energy, from 2004–2011, they learned that the companies had illegally dumped slurry containing dangerous chemicals into abandoned mines. Although state agencies could have cracked down on this, they never did. So the residents took matters into their own hands. Their lawsuit claimed that the slurry seeped into the groundwater, polluting the tap water. The plaintiffs received an undisclosed settlement before the case went to court.

Contaminated water is not just a problem in coal country. In Illinois, Kansas, Missouri, and Indiana, some drinking water has pesticides at

concentrations that are associated with birth defects and infertility. In New Jersey, New York, Arizona, and Massachusetts, drinking water contains the dry-cleaning solvent tetrachlorethylene, which may cause kidney damage and cancer. The Minnesota Department

Sherry Vargson of Granville Summit, Pennsylvania, is able to ignite her tap water, which was polluted with methane during the process of extracting natural gas, or fracking.

of Health has declared nitrate, which is particularly harmful to babies, to be a common groundwater contaminant.

While polluted water is a problem worldwide, this book will focus on issues in the United States. Since the Clean Water Act passed in 1972, America has been considered a leader in clean water. However, polluted water is not a problem of the past. According to the *New York Times*, one in ten Americans has been exposed to unsafe drinking water. In addition to drinking water, polluted water can impact swimming, fishing, and wildlife areas. The Environmental Protection Agency (EPA) reports that 35 percent of American stream miles, 45 percent of lakes, ponds, and reservoirs, and 44 percent of estuary square miles are impaired.

The EPA and state agencies regulate and enforce clean water policy. However, court decisions limiting the scope of the law, over-taxed resources, and political pressure can tie the hands of agency workers. Also, some Americans rely on well water. When the wells are private, owners must ensure the safety of their own water. For these reasons, citizens must advocate for clean water and be watchdogs for activities affecting water safety.

Good water supports its intended uses. Intended uses can include drinking, recreation, irrigation, or maintaining aquatic life. Water that doesn't support its purpose is polluted. In addition to dangerous chemicals such as those described above, polluted water may contain harmful bacteria, protozoans, viruses, or algae.

Our bodies are at least 65 percent water. We rely on water for our organs to function properly. If you ingest polluted water or eat an animal that has ingested it, you can become very sick. Swimming in polluted water can also make you ill. Where you live, clean drinking water may be readily available. However, clean water is not a given. People break rules, make mistakes, and sometimes don't have the resources to fix problems they know about. You must educate yourself about your local water. If it is polluted, advocate for it being cleaned up. When citizens raise concerns, those concerns often become a priority.

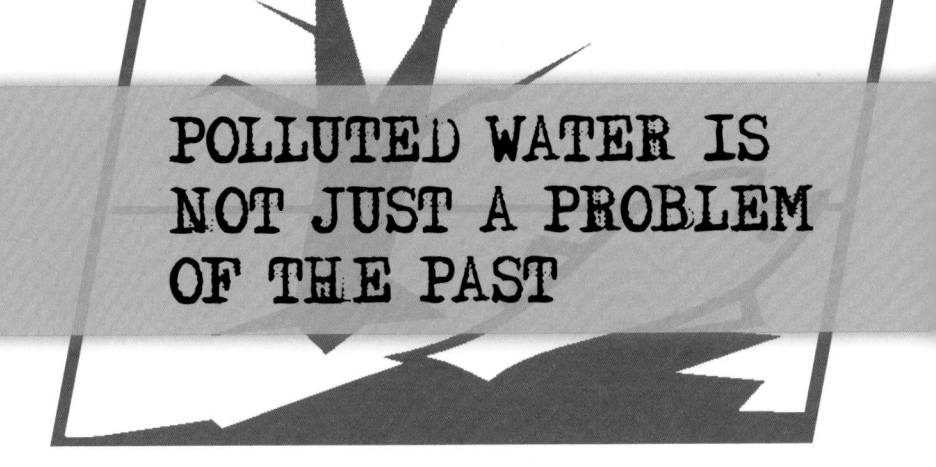

1 POLLUTED WATER IS NOT JUST A PROBLEM OF THE PAST

Many environmental factors affect the safety of water. These are grouped into point source and non-point source pollution. Point source comes from a single source, such as a factory or wastewater treatment plant. Non-point source comes from runoff or seepage occurring over a larger area. Improper disposal of industrial waste is one example of point source pollution. Industries that generate waste such as grease, oil, and toxic chemicals must dispose of it properly. Companies typically have on-site water treatment systems, or systems that remove toxic waste before it goes to a municipal water treatment center. Today, many companies do a good job of this cleanup. They use bacteria to break down toxins. They use chemistry to filter out other harmful chemicals. At times, the water they recycle back into streams is cleaner than the water they took out.

In the past, companies often improperly disposed of waste on the ground or in rivers. The waste polluted the water and made many people very sick. Congress passed the Clean Water Act in 1972 to crack down. In 1980, Congress also established the Superfund Program to clean up areas with polluted water and soil. Some companies have been tracked down to pay for the cleanups. Other times, responsible parties are difficult to find because the pollution occurred decades ago.

One Superfund site in which drinking water was polluted is in Woburn, Massachusetts, where many residents developed leukemia in the 1970s. A lawsuit resulted in the early 1980s, which is chronicled in the book *A Civil Action* by Jonathan Harr. It was later

Many large companies have their own wastewater treatment plants, like this one at the General Motors Orion Assembly Plant. Treatment plants remove toxic chemicals from the water.

made into a movie. Victims did not get a large settlement from the defendants, W. R. Grace & Company and Beatrice Foods. However, the EPA later determined that the two companies were to blame. The agency said the companies improperly disposed of trichloroethylene and perchloroethylene, compounds believed to cause leukemia. The toxic chemicals seeped into the groundwater, which was pumped for drinking water through two of the city's wells. The Superfund cleanup continues to this day.

There are many such examples of Superfund sites in which water was impaired. It is easy to look at industrial water pollution as a problem of the past. Unfortunately, that's not the case. While the United States has made strides in tackling industrial pollution in the past thirty years, court rulings have limited the scope of the Clean Water Act. Until recently, the act protected navigable waters, which was interpreted to mean most lakes and streams. Lately, however, U.S. Supreme Court rulings have interpreted navigable waters to be systems connected to larger systems. That means the EPA cannot prosecute companies polluting smaller water systems with carcinogens and bacteria, even if that pollution affects drinking water. the *New York Times* estimates that this interpretation of the law could affect the drinking water of 117 million Americans.

As an example, in 2007, McWane, Inc., an Alabama pipe manufacturer, dumped oil, lead, and zinc into a creek. At first, the company was fined millions of dollars. The decision was later overturned because of the interpretation of "navigable." Some businesses have lobbied for a narrower interpretation of the law for this exact reason: to avoid fines. The EPA would like a broader interpretation of the law. The agency is working to clarify which waters it can protect.

In the last five years, chemical factories, manufacturing plants, and other companies have violated water pollution laws more than five hundred thousand times, according to the *New York Times*. While some violations were minor, others included illegally dumping toxins that could cause cancer, birth defects, and other health problems. Even with the Clean Water Act, state agencies and the EPA often do not prosecute offenders because they either don't have a resources or they have been told not to for political reasons. Many of the companies that pollute water are seen as essential to a state's economy or to political leaders' campaign financing.

Another single point source of pollution is sewage. Many sewage systems were built more than one hundred years ago. They simply can't handle the increased flow of water due to growing populations and development. With development comes more paved ground. Rather than seeping through the soil and into the groundwater, rain-water washes into storm drains. Sewer and storm water drains are often linked, so that when it rains, the sewage overflows.

Upgrades in the 1970s and 1980s (thanks to the Clean Water Act) helped to update sewage and storm water systems at the time, but today the systems are still outdated. Nationwide, 9,400 of 25,000 sewage systems have dumped untreated waste into rivers and lakes, according to the *New York Times*. Sometimes these spills contaminate the drinking water. Sewage contains

microorganisms that can make people sick. Nausea, diarrhea, and sore throats are a few problems they can cause. An estimated twenty million people get sick from drinking water each year, according to the *New York Times*, and children and the elderly are especially susceptible. Unfortunately, cities strapped for cash can't afford to fix their water systems. However, as old pipes deteriorate and development and populations continue to rise, cities may have to increase citizens' water bills in order to tackle the dated systems.

Coal: Out of the Air and into the Water

Power plants are another source of water pollution. To reduce the coal emissions released into the air, some coal companies have begun scrubbing their air emissions. That wastewater is then filtered into nearby waterways. Some residents and lawmakers don't think the water is filtered enough. It may still allow dangerous levels of arsenic, boron, iron, manganese, cadmium, magnesium, and barium into the water. Many of these can cause cancer and other diseases. The *New York Times* reports that 90 percent of 313 coal-fired plants

WARNING

COMBINED SEWER OVERFLOW DISCHARGE POINT

POLLUTION MAY OCCUR

have violated the Clean Water Act since 2004.

Spills have also occurred. In October 2000, 300 million gallons of coal slurry were released when a Massey Energy impoundment broke in Martin County, Kentucky. The spillage flooded people's yards with up to 7 feet (2 meters) of sludge, killed all the fish in two local streams, and damaged 60 miles (97 kilometers) of river used for drinking water, according to the *Charleston Gazette*. There are many such impoundments in the Appalachia area.

Thirty-five percent of American stream miles are polluted. The Anacostia River, in Maryland and Washington, D.C., is one of America's most polluted rivers, but cleanup efforts are underway.

FRACKING: FRIEND OR FOE

Hydraulic fracturing, also known as fracking, is the process of injecting deep shale with chemicals, water, and sand, which fractures the shale and releases natural gas to be stored as energy. Natural gas has been heralded as an alternative to oil and coal. However, when fracking occurs near drinking water sources, it may contaminate that water. That is what the EPA suspects happened in Pavillion, Wyoming. There, it found chemicals linked to fracking in an aquifer used for drinking water. Residents were encouraged to seek alternative water for drinking and cooking. The EPA is now conducting a nationwide study on how fracking may affect drinking water.

As we saw earlier, sludge deposited in abandoned mines may seep into the groundwater, polluting wells. The same can happen when waste from power plants is deposited at landfills. Even with linings, the waste sometimes seeps through, polluting groundwater. A 2007 EPA report said that people living near power plant landfills had a cancer risk two thousand times higher than federal health standards. The EPA hopes to tighten rules on power plants.

Another energy source that can cause single point water pollution is oil. The world consumes 89 million barrels of oil per day, with the United States being the leading consumer. One barrel equals 42 U.S. gallons (159 liters). In contrast, the United States produces only 9.7 million barrels of oil per day, according to CNN's *Money*. Some lawmakers believe that producing more oil domestically will make America less reliant on foreign oil and stronger economically. The U.S. Energy Information Administration estimates that an additional 500,000 barrels per day could eventually be attained by opening new areas for offshore drilling. Some legislators are pushing for this. The problem is oil spills. These can occur during drilling or transport. The *Exxon Valdez* spill in 1989 occurred while the tanker was transporting oil to California. It crashed into Prince William Sound's Bligh Reef, spilling 260,000–750,000 barrels of oil. The National Transportation Safety Board (NTSB) found that there was plenty of blame to go around, including an intoxicated captain, an understaffed and exhausted crew, and a broken radar system.

The *Exxon Valdez* was the largest U.S. oil spill for two decades. On April 20, 2010, an explosion occurred on British Petroleum's oil drilling rig Deepwater Horizon. Eleven people died, 17 were injured, and 4.9 million barrels of oil spilled into the Gulf of Mexico—nineteen times the amount spilled by the *Exxon Valdez*, according to *Popular Mechanics*. The spill was due to a combination of human and technical errors. Unfortunately, BP had no backup plan in place should such a spill occur in deep water—5,000 feet (1,524 meters) in this case. A backup plan still doesn't exist. What is currently available would still allow the flow of hundreds of

thousands of barrels of oil, according to the *New York Times*. The U.S. agency that oversees offshore drilling, Minerals Management Service, has come under fire because offshore accident rates are higher in the United States than in Australia, the United Kingdom, Norway, and Canada. Agency officials have said they need more funding in order to be effective. Whether that will happen before or after another oil spill remains to be seen.

The *Exxon Valdez* crash in 1989 caused 260,000–750,000 barrels of oil to spill into the Pacific. The 2010 explosion on the Deepwater Horizon oil rig created an even larger spill of 4.9 million barrels.

2 WASHED AWAY?

Non-point source pollution comes from cumulative runoff into surface water and seepage into groundwater. Sources include roads, lawns, and farms. Runoff is probably the biggest source of water pollution in America today. Runoff is material that washes from dry land into surface water (above-ground water, such as streams, lakes, and oceans.) This process is as old as rivers themselves. Today, human activity causes dirt, bacteria, nutrients, and hazardous chemicals to inundate our waters.

Dirt, loose dust, and soil are major culprits in water pollution. While it's normal for bodies of water to contain some dirt, too much can clog fish gills, smother fish eggs, and cloud the water so that plants don't get sunlight. Excess dirt runoff is caused by disturbing the land. This happens when fields are tilled or construction projects are built.

In addition to the problems above, the dirt may be contaminated with dangerous chemicals, such as the pesticide DDT and the industrial chemical polychlorinated biphenyl (PCB.) These

were banned in the 1970s but persist in the soil. Small bottom feeders, such as worms, crustaceans, and larvae, ingest the contaminated dirt that has settled to the bottom. Larger fish eat them. They can develop fin rot, tumors, and more. Eating the contaminated fish is of course unhealthy for humans. It can cause cancer or neurological defects. For this reason, 4,598 fish consumption advisories were issued in 2010 alone, according to the EPA. The advisories covered 42 percent of U.S. lake acreage and 36 percent of river miles.

Storm drains lead to waterways, such as bays and streams. Signs like this discourage people from throwing trash or pouring harmful fluids into the drain. However, trash still washes from the street into the drain.

Residents don't always heed the advice. Sometimes Superfund sites arise out of concern for people eating locally caught fish. New Bedford Harbor, Massachusetts, is one example. In that case, PCBs pollute the water due to improper disposal of toxic waste by electrical device manufacturers many years ago.

Runoff can also contain animal manure. Some bacteria in water is normal, but runoff from stockyards and manure used as fertilizer can inundate waterways with harmful bacteria. If the runoff enters well water, it can make those who drink the water sick. The nutrients in the waste are also a problem. Animal manure is used as fertilizer

Manure runoff is a major source of water pollution. It contains nitrogen and phosphorous, which pollute streams and lakes, and in some cases well water.

for crops and residential yards because it is high in phosphorous and nitrogen. These nutrients help plants grow. (Artificial fertilizer contains the same nutrients.) When it rains or when snow melts, nitrogen and phosphorus from the fertilizer wash from field to stream or from lawn to storm drain to stream. There the nutrients help algae to grow. This can result in large algal blooms. This leads to low oxygen levels (called eutrophication), which can kill fish.

Some algal blooms can be dangerous. Some cyanobacteria (also called blue-green algae) can produce toxins. It is harmful for animals or humans to drink or cook with water containing algae, even after boiling or filtering it. Fish and shellfish exposed to algal blooms cannot be eaten. The toxic blooms have occurred at least since biblical times. While they aren't caused by pollution, nutrients in fertilizer have made the blooms larger and more abundant. Also, some harmful algae, such as *Pfiesteria*, thrive in polluted water.

Other agricultural polluters are pesticides and weed killers. Weed killers such as Atrazine can run off crops just as fertilizer does. It then travels into waterways. If it enters wells or public drinking systems, it may cause birth defects, low birth weight, and menstrual problems.

Trash and vehicle fluids are also runoff polluters. Drinking cups, plastic bags, water bottles, toys, shoes, and more are discarded outside. This trash blows or washes into storm drains, into streams, and eventually into the ocean. Oil and gas leaked from vehicles or improperly disposed of in driveway storm drains also washes into streams.

TEST YOUR WELL WATER

If you have a private well, you are responsible for testing it. Have a licensed, state-certified lab test your well water at least once a year—usually in the spring. The well should also be tested after flooding, when there is a known threat, such as waste that may seep into the groundwater, or if its taste, smell, or appearance changes. The water should be tested for total coliform bacteria, nitrates, total dissolved solids, and pH levels. Ask your local health department if there are other contaminants to be concerned about. For example, if your region is known to have groundwater polluted by pesticides, have that tested. Volatile organic compounds, which are fuel-related contaminants, may also be a concern. If you think your well water is contaminated, do not drink it. Contact your health department for advice.

In the past, local streams were a fun place to cool off on a summer day. Now, swimming in some streams can be like swimming in garbage. The trash travels from stream to ocean. In the ocean, it moves in gyres, systems of giant circular pathways. These gyres carry trash and eventually deposit it onto beaches. Some of the trash remains trapped in the gyres, as is the case with the Great Pacific Garbage Patch, a sea of trash estimated to be as large as the state of Texas.

The runoff pollution problem is compounded by impervious ground. As population grows, so does development. Soil and vegetation are paved over for parking lots, driveways, and roads. These provide a faster and less absorbent track for oils, trash, and more to wash into gutters, culverts, and storm drains. They then wash into streams and wetlands. Streams have also been altered, making the water flow faster, cutting down on plant growth. Wetlands have been drained for developments. These were natural filtering systems for water. Just when water needs the most filtering, that system is impaired.

In Oxon Cove along the Potomac River, plastic bottles litter the shore. Blankets of trash like this are not uncommon sights along the shores of U.S. rivers.

Seeping Giants

Unlike surface water, you don't see groundwater, but it's very important. Half the U.S. population relies on groundwater for drinking. When rain and snow fall on unpaved surfaces, the water seeps into the ground. Moving downward, it reaches an area saturated with water. This is groundwater. The groundwater is mixed with solid matter like rocks and sand. Groundwater that can be pumped through a well is called an aquifer. Pollutants on the ground or underground can seep into the groundwater, and into people's well water.

Groundwater can be polluted by buried fuel tanks (on properties where oil is used for heat) and at gas stations. Leaky septic systems are also to blame. Pesticides, chemicals spilled on the ground, and harmful chemicals from improperly lined landfills can all seep into groundwater.

Animal manure is another culprit. This is mainly a problem on very large farms or feedlots (sometimes called factory farms). To dispose of their animal manure, these farmers spray it onto their fields. A large dairy farm, with 1,400 cows, can produce 1.5 million gallons (5.7 million liters) of manure a month, according to the *New York Times*. If it's spread too thickly over surrounding acreage, it can seep into the groundwater and impair the well water. Those who drink or bathe in the well water may become sick due to harmful bacteria or protozoa in the water. Young children and the elderly are especially susceptible. This type of pollution wasn't addressed by the Clean Water Act. Residents must monitor the safety of their private wells.

3 YOU ARE WHAT YOU DRINK

As you know, drinking clean water is good for your health. Water makes up about two-thirds of your body weight and is essential to every system in your body. It moistens tissues in your mouth, eyes, and nose; lubricates your joints; regulates body temperature; flushes waste from your kidneys and liver; and carries oxygen and nutrients to your cells. Unfortunately, the fact that water plays such an important role in your essential organs means that bad water can wreak havoc on your body.

First, let's look at harmful microorganisms. These live in raw sewage and animal manure. When these things contaminate drinking water, microorganisms can become a threat to your health. The three main microorganisms living in unclean water are bacteria, protozoans, and viruses.

Bacteria are not always bad. In fact, you have some helpful bacteria living in your digestive system right now. They actually help with digestion. However, other bacteria, such as some species of *Escherichia coli* (*E. coli*), produce harmful toxins that damage your cells and can make you sick. *E. coli*, for instance, can cause diarrhea. Your body is constantly producing new cells, which is why you can usually recover from these sicknesses. Doctors sometimes prescribe antibiotics to kill harmful bacteria when people get serious illnesses.

Protozoans are single-celled organisms that behave like animals. Like bacteria, some protozoans live peacefully in your digestive system. Others are harmful. (Malaria is a commonly known disease caused by protozoans. It is transmitted through mosquitoes.)

Microorganisms such as the *E. coli* bacteria in this petri dish live in raw sewage and animal manure. If you drink or swim in polluted water, microorganisms can enter your body.

One protozoan sometimes found in water is *Giardia lamblia*. When you drink water contaminated with *Giardia*, you ingest cysts, which are dormant protozoans. Your stomach acid causes trophozoites to emerge from the cysts. These attach to the walls of your small intestines, causing cramps and diarrhea. Medicine is usually prescribed to attack the protozoans and clear up the infection.

Viruses are less than single cells. They are DNA or RNA sequences, which give instructions for cell activity. Viruses invade healthy cells so that they no longer operate correctly. The body has ways of fighting many viruses. Antivirus medications may be prescribed. But often, you just have to let the viral infection run its course and treat your symptoms. For instance, if you have a stomach virus, you may take over-the-counter medicine to fight nausea. The medicine makes you feel better, but it does not directly attack the virus. Viruses found in drinking water can cause diarrhea, vomiting, cramps, and sore throat.

Not all microorganisms are harmful. But some bacteria, protozoans, and viruses found in polluted water can make you sick. Sometimes the illness can be serious.

If you are a healthy teen, you will likely recover from these illnesses. However, you may feel sick for a couple of weeks. This may result in missed school and work. Still, it's important to rest so that you can recover. In order to recover more quickly, it helps to take care of yourself. Seek ways to reduce stress. Eat healthy, exercise, get plenty of sleep, and don't smoke or use harmful drugs. Then your body will be better able to fight infections. Very young children, elderly people, and people with chronic illnesses are hit hardest by these diseases, as their immune systems are not as equipped to fight them. If you've visited a newborn in the hospital, you likely washed your hands directly before holding him or her. That's why!

Next, we'll look at how water contaminated with harmful chemicals can affect your body. When swallowed, the chemicals are digested and taken up into your bloodstream, where they are carried to your major organs, including your brain, liver, kidneys, and reproductive organs. You may feel the effects of exposure right away, as sickness or dizziness. Or they may have a cumulative effect later.

In high doses, arsenic is a deadly poison. It's also poisonous in lower doses over time. It damages cells and creates a shortage of white and red blood cells, causing weakness and lowered immunity. Arsenic can occur naturally in water. However, high levels are often due to pesticide use in the past. In the short term, arsenic can cause skin discoloration and lesions, "pins and needles" feelings in hands and feet, nausea, and weakness. In the long term, it causes lung, skin, kidney, liver, and bladder cancer. Interestingly, despite these potential effects, arsenic is an effective chemotherapy (anti-cancer) medication used to treat a certain type of leukemia.

Lead can be caused by eroding lead pipes or by industry pollution. (Aside from water pollution, exposure is often due to old paint, which contained lead.) It is distributed throughout the body in the same manner as helpful nutrients such as calcium. Instead of helping the body, it damages it. In the bloodstream, it damages red blood cells, causing anemia. In the bones, it interferes with calcium,

In Picher, Oklahoma, in 2008, the river ran red with heavy metals and toxic chemicals, legacies of lead and zinc mining. The town is a Superfund site.

weakening the bones. It can also affect the nervous system, leading to learning disabilities and attention disorders.

Tetrachlorethylene, a by-product of dry cleaning, is stored in body fat and released slowly into the bloodstream. In the short term, it can cause headache, sleepiness, confusion, and nausea. In the long term, it can damage the nervous system and may cause liver and kidney damage.

While nitrates occur naturally in water, too high a concentration can pose health risks. This is a problem where animal manure or artificial fertilizer runs off or seeps into drinking water. For all ages, it may increase the risk of cancer over time. However, most known risks are to babies and pregnant or nursing mothers. Babies who drink nitrate polluted water or have it mixed in their formula can develop blue baby syndrome, so named because the skin appears blue, especially around the eyes, nose, and mouth. It is the symptom of a serious problem called methemoglobinemia, due to a lack of oxygen in the blood. It must be treated immediately and can be fatal.

The EPA regulates the above microorganisms and chemicals, and many others. A full list is available on the agency's Web site. However, laws have not been updated to include potentially dangerous chemicals, or to regulate mixtures of multiple chemicals occurring in drinking water. Regulations that do exist often aren't followed. Each year, 19.5 million Americans still get sick from drinking water contaminated with microorganisms. In 2008, 40 percent

From Sea to Plastic Sea

Plastic is a major polluter of the world's oceans. Look around your house and school. You'll likely see a lot of plastic—much of it disposable. When discarded, it can blow from land to water, where it is weathered, but not fully biodegraded. It is broken down into ever smaller pieces of plastic, which float in our oceans and settle to the bottom. Fish and other marine animals eat the plastics. This fills them up so that they don't eat real food. Then they die. Some parts of the ocean have higher concentrations of plastics than others. These are often called garbage patches.

of public water systems violated the Safe Drinking Water Act. While some violations were minor, others polluted drinking water with harmful chemicals.

Swimming in Dirty Waters

In some ways, swimming in polluted water is like drinking it. You typically swallow small sips of water while swimming. When you swim in water contaminated by microorganisms, they can attack your body through the swallowed water or through your nose.

This can cause stomachaches. If they get into your ear, they can cause ear infections such as swimmer's ear. They can also cause pink eye or a skin rash. On the other hand, you may not get sick at all from swimming in water polluted with microorganisms. Your body may fight them off without you even knowing it.

Likewise, swimming in water containing toxic chemicals can lead to the chemicals entering your body through your mouth, nose, or skin. Your skin is your largest organ. It protects your body from

A sign at Will Rogers State Beach in Pacific Palisades, California, advises people not to swim. There were high bacteria levels near a storm drain. Nationwide, pollution caused twenty-five thousand beach closings or swim advisories in 2007.

some harmful chemicals. Others can be absorbed. Algal blooms can also be toxic to swimmers. Swimming in water with thick algae may cause a rash, vomiting, diarrhea, and shortness of breath.

Oil spills also create unsafe swimming conditions. If the water smells like oil (like a gas station) or if you can see oil, the EPA recommends that you not swim in that water. Oil contains benzene, which can cause cancer, and hydrocarbons, which can cause sickness and respiratory problems. When visitors flee the shoreline, local economies slow down. People are unable to make a living. After an oil spill, the shores needn't be abandoned forever. In time, the oil weathers, and the toxins are diluted.

Of course, humans aren't the only creatures harmed by polluted waters. All of this pollution affects wildlife, too. If you've seen photos of seabirds covered in oil after a spill, you know how devastating pollution can be for marine animals. As water gets more polluted, more animal and human populations will be affected.

4 WHAT CAN YOU DO?

Jennifer Hall-Massey and the other coal slurry plaintiffs in West Virginia saw their neighbors get sick. They saw that their water didn't look right. They gathered information. They learned from West Virginia University researchers that the same chemicals in coal slurry were in their water. They learned that coal companies had self-reported to state regulators the dumping of illegal amounts of toxins into the ground. Next they took action. They sued coal companies for the contamination. They also asked legislators to make stricter laws about slurry disposal. They probably did not plan on dedicating several years of their lives to fighting for clean water. However, they took the time to make things right. It is up to each of us to advocate for clean water in our communities.

The first step is to be informed. Read your area's Drinking Water Quality Report (sometimes called the Consumer Confidence Report). This is provided by your local water supplier. Also read your state's Source Water Assessment, which

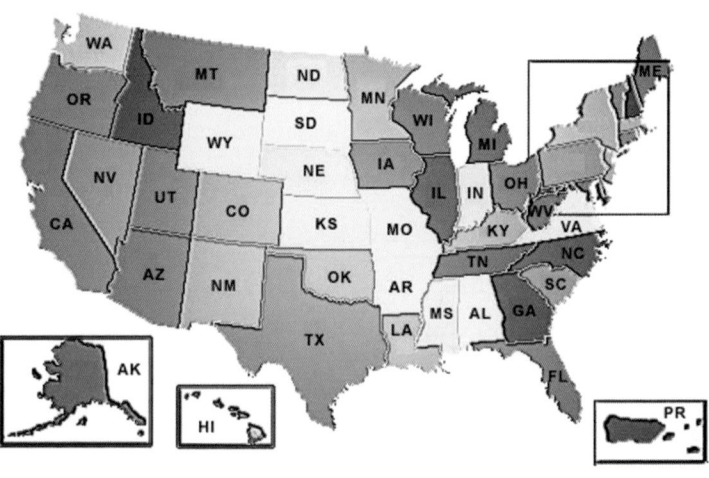

EPA United States Environmental Protection Agency

Advanced Search   A–Z

LEARN THE ISSUES   SCIENCE & TECHNOLOGY   LAWS & REGULATIONS   ABOUT EPA

Water: Local Drinking Water Information   ✉Contact Us

You are here: Water » Drinking Water » Local Drinking Water Information

Local Drinking Water Information

Water Home

Drinking Water
 Analytical Methods and
  Laboratories
 Consumer Information
 Drinking Water Standards
 Emergency Preparedness
 Local Drinking Water
  Information
 Private Wells
 Virtual Tour of Water
  Treatment Plant
 Water Contaminants
 Water Security
 Water on Tap:
  Consumer's Guide

Education & Training

Grants & Funding

Laws & Regulations

Our Waters

Pollution Prevention &
Control

Resources & Performance

Science & Technology

Water Infrastructure

What You Can Do

Each year by July 1 you should receive in the mail a short report (consumer confidence report, or drinking water qual
report) from your water supplier that tells where your water comes from and what's in it:

- see if your annual drinking water quality report is posted on-line,
- read some frequent questions about these reports, or
- find states participating in Drinking Water Watch.

*Note: The external links to state web sites and contacts may not be accurate at this time, we are currently reviewing
information. Please check back with us for the updates on these pages.*

**To find information about your local drinking water system,
select a state or zoom in on the Northeast.**

Follow links below to the state and local members of our safe drinking water partner organizations:

American Water Works Association EXIT Disclaimer

Association of Metropolitan Water Agencies EXIT Disclaimer

The EPA provides information about local drinking water on its Web site. It
advocates for clean drinking water and prosecutes companies that are guilty
of water pollution.

will tell of pollutants in waters that feed your drinking water supply. Read the newspaper and pay attention to activities that may affect your water. Attend meetings regarding construction and other activities. Ask what will be done to ensure that these activities do not pollute your local water. If your water comes from a private well, cistern, or spring, your family must protect your water source. Test your water, maintain your well, and be aware of activities that affect the surrounding groundwater.

If there is a problem, be a reporter. Report polluted water or activities that could endanger your area's water supply. You can report illegal activities (such as illegal disposal of waste) to police. Polluted water can be reported to state agencies. You can also report problems to the media, which tends to bring prompt action by local authorities. Follow up. If nobody responds, report it until somebody does. It's also important to share information with community members. The more voices, the better.

Next, take action. Support clean water efforts. Your area may have a "stream team"—a group that picks up trash around streams before it washes into the water. Learn about clean water efforts by nonprofits, universities, and businesses, and get involved. You can also take steps to decrease your effect on water. Avoid buying heavily packaged foods and disposable containers, such as water bottles, which can wash into our waterways. If you do use disposable goods, recycle them to reduce the pollution caused during manufacturing. Reduce gasoline emissions by walking or riding a bike. Conserve energy by shutting down computers and other electronics at night, turning off lights, and not overheating or over-cooling your house.

Keep pesticide and fertilizer use to a minimum or avoid using them altogether. If you have a lawn business, consider being environmentally friendly. By learning how to care for lawns without pesticides and fertilizers, you may find a new niche. Keep your car tuned to avoid oil and gas leaks. If your family owns a boat, keep the motors tuned, as well. Clean the boat with nontoxic soap.

In your home, use nontoxic cleanser whenever possible. For instance, you can use vinegar and water to clean countertops and floors. Dispose of household chemicals properly. The following

Aimee Code and her nineteen-month-old, Hayley, have an organic garden in Eugene, Oregon. Since pesticides wash from yards to streams, it's best not to use pesticides or fertilizer in order to cut down on water pollution.

shouldn't be flushed, washed down the drain, or disposed of in a storm drain: cleaners, beauty products, diapers, feminine products, medicine, paint, lawn care products, grease, and vehicle fluids. (A single quart of motor oil poured into a driveway storm drain can contaminate two million gallons of drinking water.) Many of the items above should be thrown in the trash or recycled when possible. Used oil should be recycled. Hazardous waste, such as pesticides, oil-based paint, batteries, and solvents, should be taken to a designated hazardous waste facility.

What Are Others Doing?

As an advocate for clean water, you won't be alone. Others have a common vision. Some are legislators or government workers. Congress created the Clean Water Act, and federal regulations have banned some of the most harmful chemicals from industrial and agricultural use. The EPA and state environmental agencies have the authority to enforce the Clean Water Act. They look to citizens to be partners in advocating for clean water.

Independent groups are also taking action. They include the Groundwater Foundation, the American Ground Water Trust, and the Natural Resources Conservation Service. There are also grassroots groups, which often focus on a specific problem or goal. They include the Coal River Mountain Watch in West Virginia. It takes action against pollution by coal companies. It has arranged for emergency drinking water for citizens, lobbied for the state agency

BE A CLEAN WATER TEAM

You don't have to do it all yourself. Here are some ideas for getting friends, classmates, and neighbors involved in ensuring clean water for your community.

- Organize a trash cleanup in your neighborhood.
- Stencil signs on storm drains, indicating that they lead to streams and should not be used for waste disposal.
- Lead a public service campaign at your school. Hang posters educating students about ways to keep pollutants out of waterways.
- If your area has clean drinking water, spread the word. Let people know that filling a water bottle from the tap is more environmentally friendly than drinking water from disposable bottles.
- If your drinking water is unclean, organize a community meeting to share information. Contact the local media to cover the event.

to take action, and brought the issue of polluted water to national attention through the *New York Times*.

Farms and businesses also play a role in clean water. Some have changed their practices to be more environmentally friendly. Construction companies reduce soil runoff by fencing construction sites. Farmers fence grazing areas so that animal waste won't

pollute streams and plant grass instead of leaving fields fallow to avoid soil runoff.

Cities are also making a difference. Located on the Puget Sound, Tacoma, Washington, was once home to waterfront factories and mills that polluted the water. After a multimillion-dollar Superfund cleanup, the city redesigned its waterfront. It is now home to clean water research institutes and ecofriendly businesses.

Volunteers clean Watts Branch Stream, a tributary of the Anacostia River, which spans Maryland and Washington, D.C. The EPA estimates that 20,000 tons (18,144 metric tons) of trash flow into the Anacostia each year.

The Center for Urban Waters studies and implements ways to restore health to coastal waters. The Port of Tacoma, a major U.S. shipping hub, has cleaned up 420 acres (1.7 square km) and restored 80 acres (.3 square km) of wildlife habitat and now considers the potential environmental impact of its decision making.

Our streams, lakes, and ocean waters are some of our most precious resources. If we don't pitch in to make them cleaner and ask our leaders to make this a priority, they will only get more polluted as population grows. America's drinking water, as a whole, is among the cleanest in the world. Citizens have worked hard for, and at times fought for, that clean water. Most drinking water is clean. However, clean drinking water isn't something that should be taken for granted. There are unscrupulous people, and mistakes are made, resulting in unclean drinking water and devastating health effects. Watchdog efforts are needed to discourage wrongdoing. Past and present examples show that we can't afford to be complacent. We all must advocate for clean water.

MYTHS & FACTS

Myth: Polluted drinking water is a problem of the past.

Fact: While many companies and organizations have worked hard to clean up drinking water, pollution can still be found.

Myth: Polluted water contains harmful chemicals.

Fact: Polluted water can contain chemicals. It may also contain microorganisms from raw sewage or manure.

Myth: Toxic algae blooms are caused by pollution.

Fact: Toxic algae blooms have existed for thousands of years. However, they are exacerbated by pollution from fertilizer.

10 GREAT QUESTIONS TO ASK AN ENVIRONMENTALIST

1. **Who is responsible for testing my drinking water?**
2. **How do I access the results of those tests?**
3. **What is the water quality in local streams and lakes?**
4. **What issues in my area could contribute to water pollution?**
5. **What can I do to reduce water pollution?**
6. **What can I do to advocate for clean water?**
7. **What groups are working toward clean water in our area?**
8. **What careers are there involving clean water?**
9. **What is the most pressing goal in reducing water pollution in America?**
10. **What is the state of clean drinking water around the world?**

GLOSSARY

algae Simple one-celled organisms that often live in water or damp areas.

bacteria A type of single-celled organism.

estuary The area where a stream or river meets the ocean, and fresh water and saltwater mingle.

fertilizer Nutrients, as from manure or chemicals, that help plants to grow.

groundwater The water that trickles through the ground and into a saturated zone underground.

microorganisms Living things so small that they can be seen only with a microscope.

nitrate A compound found in manure and artificial fertilizers.

protozoans Single-celled parasites that often live in water.

runoff Rain or other water that washes off land and into bodies of water.

sewage Wastewater flushed or washed down the drain and into a water system.

slurry The wastewater from processing coal.

surface water Above-ground water, such as lakes or streams.

virus A DNA or RNA sequence, usually housed within a protein coat, that hijacks a cell.

FOR MORE INFORMATION

Clean Water Action

111 New Montgomery Street, # 600

San Francisco, CA 94105

(415) 369-9160

Web site: http://www.cleanwateraction.org

Clean Water Action works to clean up America's waters by holding polluters accountable and supporting renewable energy.

Clean Water Foundation

80 St. Clair Avenue West, Suite 10

Toronto, ON M4V 1N3

Canada

(416) 425-1313

Web site: http://www.cleanwaterfoundation.org

The Clean Water Foundation works with other organizations to create policies and practices supporting clean water in Canada.

Groundwater Foundation

P.O. Box 22558

Lincoln, NE 68542-2558

(800) 858-4844 or (402) 434-2740

Web site: http://www.groundwater.org

The Groundwater Foundation educates people and organizes community action for sustainable, clean groundwater.

Water Project, Inc.
P.O. Box 3353
Concord, NH 03302-3353
(800) 460-8974
Web site: http://thewaterproject.org
*The Water Project brings clean water to those throughout the world who do not
have it.*

Web Sites

Due to the changing nature of Internet links, Rosen Publishing has
developed an online list of Web sites related to the subject of this
book. This site is updated regularly. Please use this link to access the list:

http://www.rosenlinks.com/IDE/Orgs

FOR FURTHER READING

Bang, Molly. *Nobody Particular: One Woman's Fight to Save the Bays*. New York, NY: Holt, 2000.

Calhoun, Yael, ed. *Water Pollution* (Environmental Issues). New York, NY: Chelsea House, 2005.

Fridell, Ron. *Protecting Earth's Water Supply*. Minneapolis, MN: Lerner, 2009.

Gates, Alexander, and Robert Blauvelt. *Encyclopedia of Pollution*. Vol. 1 and 2. New York, NY: Facts On File, 2011.

Gold, Susan Dudley. *Clean Air and Clean Water Acts* (Landmark Legislation). Tarrytown, NY: Marshall Cavendish, 2011.

Hiassen, Carl. *Flush*. New York, NY: Yearling, 2010.

Kennedy, Brian, ed. *Water* (Issues That Concern You). Farmington Hills, MI: Greenhaven, 2011.

LaBella, Laura. *Not Enough to Drink: Pollution, Drought, and Tainted Water Supplies*. New York, NY: Rosen, 2009.

Landau, Elaine. *Oil Spill: Disaster in the Gulf of Mexico*. Minneapolis, MN: Lerner, 2011.

Ostopowich, Melanie. *Water Pollution* (Water Science). New York, NY: Weigl, 2010.

Savedge, Jenn. *The Green Teen: The Eco-Friendly Teen's Guide to Saving the Planet*. Gabriola Island, BC: New Society, 2009.

Stracher, Cameron. *The Water Wars*. Naperville, IL: Sourcebooks, 2011.

BIBLIOGRAPHY

Associated Press. "Judges to Review Leak of Massey Coal Slurry Deal." *Charleston Gazette*, August 23, 2011. Retrieved February 15, 2012 (http://wvgazette.com/News/201108231250).

Davis, Devra. *When Smoke Ran Like Water: Tales of Environmental Deception and the Battle Against Pollution*. New York, NY: Perseus, 2002.

Department of Labor and Industries. "Understanding Toxic Substances." Retrieved January 8, 2012 (http://www.lni.wa.gov/wisha/p-ts/pdfs/toxicsubstances.pdf).

DeVilliers, Marq. *Water: The Fate of Our Most Precious Resource*. Boston, MA: Houghton Mifflin, 2000.

Duhigg, Charles. "Toxic Waters" series. *New York Times*, August 22, 2009–March 22, 2010. Retrieved January 10, 2012 (http://projects.nytimes.com/toxic-waters).

Klucas, Gillian. *Leadville: The Struggle to Revive an American Town*. Washington, DC: Shearwater, 2004.

Medline Plus. "Drinking Water." National Library of Medicine. Retrieved January 3, 2012 (http://www.nlm.nih.gov/medlineplus/drinkingwater.html).

Ravenscroft, Peter, Hugh Brammer, and Keith Richards. *Arsenic Pollution: A Global Synthesis*. West Sussex, England: Wiley-Blackwell, 2009.

Ward, Ken, Jr. "Taking Big Coal to Task Is Difficult." *Charleston Gazette*, April 2, 2011. Retrieved January 14, 2012 (http://www.gazette.com/News/montcoal/201104020982).

INDEX

About the Author

Prior to writing for children, Bridget Heos wrote for *Missouri Lawyers Weekly,* covering a wide variety of cases, including environmental ones. Her husband's family is from Woburn, Massachusetts, site of the lawsuit depicted in *A Civil Action*. Heos is the author of more than thirty nonfiction books for children. She lives in Kansas City with her husband and three sons.

Photo Credits

Cover background vasakkohaline/Shutterstock.com; p. 5 Christian Science Monitor/Getty Images; pp. 9, 19, 28, 36 © AP Images; pp. 12–13, 22 Douglas Graham/C-Q Roll Call Group/Getty Images; p. 16 Anchorage Daily News/McClatchy-Tribune/Getty Images; p. 18 Universal Images Group/Getty Images; p. 25 Boston Globe/ Getty Images; p. 26 Jupiterimages/Polka Dot/Thinkstock; p. 31 David McNew/Getty Images; p. 39 The Washington Post/Getty Images; graphics and textures: © iStockphoto.com/stockcam (cover, back cover, interior splatters), © iStockphoto.com/Anna Chelnokova (back cover, interior splashes), © iStockphoto.com/ Dusko Jovic (back cover, p. 41 background), © iStockphoto.com/ Hadel Productions (pp. 4, 14, 21, 30, 38 text borders), © iStockphoto.com/traveler1116 (caption background texture).

Designer: Brian Garvey; Editor: Bethany Bryan;
Photo Researcher: Amy Feinberg